1 MONTH OF
FREE
READING

at

www.ForgottenBooks.com

By purchasing this book you are eligible for one month membership to ForgottenBooks.com, giving you unlimited access to our entire collection of over 1,000,000 titles via our web site and mobile apps.

To claim your free month visit:
www.forgottenbooks.com/free910631

ISBN 978-0-266-92469-2
PIBN 10910631

This book is a reproduction of an important historical work. Forgotten Books uses
state-of-the-art technology to digitally reconstruct the work, preserving the original format
whilst repairing imperfections present in the aged copy. In rare cases, an imperfection in
the original, such as a blemish or missing page, may be replicated in our edition. We do,
however, repair the vast majority of imperfections successfully; any imperfections that
remain are intentionally left to preserve the state of such historical works.

Kentucky
Birthplace Cabin

Miscellaneous Replicas

Excerpts from newspapers and other sources

From the files of the

Lincoln Financial Foundation Collection

December 13, 1928

Mr. Charles F. Southard
Speculator, New York

Dear Mr. Southard:

    I am wondering what progress you have been able
to make on the building of the Lincoln cabin at Speculator,
New York.

    In the last letter which you sent you intimated
that some progress had been made, and I am anxious to
learn what success has resulted from the project.

    In your course of inquiries I am wondering if you
came across any other facsimilies of the original Lincoln
cabin.   As far as I can learn, the one at Milton and the
one at Fort Wayne are the only two in America.

    We hope to have some detailed information about
the construction of these cabins soon, in order to encourage
their building in other parts of the country.   Any suggestions you might wish to make in respect to this would be
very gladly received.

    In your travels about the country I should be very
glad if you would keep me in touch with any Lincoln items
of historical value as our ambition is to gather as much
available material about Lincoln as possible.

    If your itinerary brings you to Fort Wayne, I hope
you will call and see me.

                    Very respectfully yours,

                    _____ Director,
LAN:VL   Lincoln Historical Research Foundation.

Called Lincoln Cabin

This log cabin, near Neosho, Mo., is more than 100 years old and is called the Lincoln Cabin. The photograph was taken by R. L. Cline, district traffic chief at Joplin.

Edith Swift, chief operator at Neosho, says the cabin gets its name from a story current in the neighborhood that Lincoln used to make visits to relatives who occupied the cabin, during his boyhood.

[20]

KEEPING FARMERS CONT[

Alfred G. Arvold Helped Solve
Economic Problem of
Checking Migration to Cities
With His Little Country
Theater Movement

By Gladys G. Feld
and Alexander Gottlieb

THE problem of keeping happy, satisfied country folk on their farms and in their tiny communities has been adequately solved in a little town in North Dakota.

A man aimed with an extraordinary vision and a bold creative power has, because of his stimulating persistence, struck a new era in communal life, and brought to it, after twenty years of ardent labor, a cultural bond which has made him famed and beloved not only in the section of the country in which he has worked but throughout the United States.

The man is Alfred G. Arvold of Fargo, N. D., and the medium through which he has brought enjoyment, knowledge and a new vital link in folk activity is the Little Country Theater, started in 1914 and still continuing its phenomenal growth.

The story of how a professor in what was once an obscure little agricultural college has become a world authority on bettering community life conditions is as romantic as fiction in its unfolding, and has its origin in a love for drama fostered in the heart of a small Wisconsin boy who vended popcorn up and down the aisles of the one crude theater in his birthplace. This love for the theater, with its roots firmly planted, was developed some

years later when the boy became a freshman at the University of Wisconsin, and not only studied but took part in plays during his college career.

Two years after he had completed his formal education and become head of the Department of Public Discussion and Social Service at the North Dakota Agricultural College, Alfred Arvold was inspired to found the Little Country Theater.

"It all began," says Mr. Arvold, "when a country school teacher wrote me for copies of some plays which were subsequently successfully staged. Her request was followed by a number of others. A careful study impressed me with the fact that a laboratory of some kind was essential, and the result was the first Little Country Theater in the world."

Physically speaking, the theater is located on the second floor of the Administration Building at Fargo, but spiritually this humanizing center is a focus point for practically every community in the world. Dedicated as it is to the discovery of talent hidden in out-of-the-way places, to giving people in the open country and villages a chance for self expression, enjoyment and relaxation, the real purpose of the movement is to make the drama an enlightening instrument which will increase culture and happiness in community life

The original Little Country Theater, once a dingy uninviting chapel, is today a cheerful country laboratory where all sorts of programs are discussed and tried out by those who flock for ideas to make life in their villages more attractive. The auditorium, with its 350 seats, corresponds to the average small town or neighborhood hall

At the right of the stage is a tower used as a study, which contains a large number of volumes on the theater and biographies of famous actors and actresses To the left of the stage and up a flight of old-fashioned stairs is the now famous Lincoln log cabin For many years it was an unused attic. Now the workshop of the theater, the cabin represents what any church basement or community hall attic may be converted into. Simplicity is its keynote.

The Lincoln cabin [?]ation from farmers clu[ ] special institutes, to groups, and it has enter[ed] the country girl who [ ] raising the biggest pig[ ] tional fame.

"Coffee and dough[ ] tomary end of every fu[ ] homely, hospitable atm[ ] and ideas are interchan[ ]

Scene from a Little Country Theater Play

Alfred G. Arvold

BROOKLYN N Y EAGLE
SEPTEMBER 1, 1929

The cabin is quaintly and tastefully furnished in the manner of nearly a century ago, and on the rough tables, spread with bright homespun linen, a hundred persons may be served comfortably. A scene laboratory opens off the main cabin, where materials are housed for building any scene desired. Here the beautiful settings used in "Peer Gynt" were painted.

Cincinnati ohio Oct 18 a.d. 1931

Dear Doctor In your writ'n of Oct 14
About The second grate man who Di...
● a grate Cause Jesus & Mr Lincoln.
Iff we had MOR MEN fowling in there
step-s. This old U.S.A wood be a bettr
for all of us. I Shall Save your writ up
Dicken Lincoln Scrap Book. as i have one.
Pay Buck pull. I have 30 Historical Fraim
pictures. In this farm Scan are 67 Objects i
Scan make up. True To life For I Spent 27 years
life on a farm The Scan is 30 inchis by 48.
in a glass Case yes it wood of bin Sold
now. Iff This grand Lesson we are Learning
not over Took ous Sale Price is $300.00 Bu
Crates & ship at his Exspence no real Lincoln
part with it for a 1000 Dollars But trying
it in younger hunds I must Sell For i am
old & growing younger Every day or at least
That way Doctor Pleas return Theas news.
● write up. & U Drive up Som after noon
Sunday Morning & See This work
I do not Know wrathr you ar Relatives of Mon...
people. dunt Nancy & uncle Elijah Warren no...
a way. but Thay wore fine People Thanks
Geo E Kincaid
1139 Draper St Cin ohio

Calvin

October 19, 1931

Mr. George L. Kincaid
1189 Draper St.
Cincinnati, Ohio

My dear Mr. Kincaid:

Thank you very much for calling to my
attention the availability of some miniature Lincoln
souvenirs you have brought together.

I remember having read about them at the
time the story appeared in the newspapers and, of
course, was interested in them.

It is to be regretted, however, that this
foundation has no available funds for the purchasing
of such Lincoln curios but I trust you may have no
difficulty in disposing of them.

My people were born and lived in Massachusetts
all of their lives and my brother and I were the first
of the family to break away and come West so I do not
expect that your relatives and mine were very closely
related.

Some time while going through Cincinnati
I would like to stop and see your collection.

Respectfully yours,

_____Director
Lincoln Historical Research Foundation

LAW:MN
L. A. Warren

CARQUINEZ SCHOOL DISTRICT
CROCKETT, CALIFORNIA

April I, 1933.

The Lincoln Historical Research Foundation
Lincoln National Life Insurance Co.
Fort Wayne, Ind.

The boys of our school are planning to make a replic
of the cabin in which Abraham Lincoln was born. We are writing to
you for the exact size of the cabin and also to know if the logs w
round or hewn. We would, indeed be very grateful if you could give
this information.

Yours respectfully

Cabin Replica

April 8, 1933

Mr. George A. Johnson, Principal
Carquines School District
Crockett, California

My dear Mr. Johnson:

I presume that you have some pictures of
the Lincoln cabin which would give you some idea
of its general appearance. The logs were hewn
and the outside measurements of the original cabin
were 18' x 20' the chimney being on the 18' side
and the door and window on the 20' side with the
chimney to the left.

The replica of the cabin which has been
erected at Hodgenville although many of the same
logs were used is much smaller than the original
cabin. The rebuilt cabin is about 14' x 18'.

We have a replica of the cabin now at Hodgenville here in Fort Wayne and there is another
at the Century of Progress Exposition at Chicago.

If we can help you further will you kindly
advise us?

Yours very sincerely,

Director
Lincoln National Life Foundation

LAW/H

Replica Of Lincoln Cabin To Go Up Here

By W. P. Turner

A replica of the log cabin in which Abraham Lincoln was born is to be built in Tyrrell park by CWA workmen, if present plans are carried out, according to Frank Bertschler, city park superintendent.

In fact, a fair proportion of the logs to be used in the building, which should become a show place for this area, already have been hewn. Among the CWA workers in Tyrrell park are two men who have had extensive experience in saw milling camps and who can wield an ax perhaps as expertly as the great emancipator himself in his best rail-splitting days. These men are Jim Barnes and Jesse Welch. J. H. Batters, superintendent for the park department, is a native of the piney woods and also has plenty of ideas about the handling and use of timber which he is eager to incorporate in the erection of a Lincoln cabin.

Bertschler said it had been suggested that it would be more in keeping with the traditions of the south to erect a Robert E. Lee memorial. But as Lee was an aristocrat and was born in a large home, it would be impracticable to try to reproduce his home, and, besides, the available timbers and the natural setting in Tyrrell park lend themselves admirably to the possibility of erecting a simple cabin of the type in which Lincoln was born, according to Bertschler. No memorial could have greater educational value to the children of the Sabine area than a Lincoln cabin, suggesting how a boy under the protection of American institutions can rise from a low station in life to the presidency, in the opinion of Bertschler.

The original Lincoln cabin in Kentucky was made of pine. The Beaumont replica will be more elaborate in the selection of materials. The only pine used will be in the roof. The ground logs will be of red oak or elm and the walls of gum. Red dirt, which is seen at various places in the district, will be hauled to the cabin site and placed in the yard. The terrain in which Lincoln was born is noted for its red earth.

Located in about the middle of the park, in full view from a winding roadway, the cabin will occupy a clearing with a background of trees. A small parking place will be provided for the convenience of visitors inspecting the cabin.

The Lincoln National Life Insurance company will donate a bust of Lincoln to be placed in the cabin arrangements being made through Dan E. Peavy, local agent.

Bertschler gained the idea of building the cabin last summer when he saw a Lincoln cabin at the World's fair. He read some books at the library about the construction of cabins of this nature, and finally contacted Peavy, who was able to provide a complete set of plans.

The dimensions of the cabin will be a width of 12 feet, length of 14 feet, and height to the edge of the eaves of 10 feet. It will have a built-up dirt floor, one window and one door.

There is more interest in the life of Lincoln in this part of Texas than one ordinarily would believe, especially among northern people coming to this section, according to Bertschler.

One Beaumont family cherishes an intimate sacred memory of the birth of the Civil war president.

A Mrs. Dearing, grandmother of Jim Rachford and Mrs. E. L. Nall, well known Beaumonters, lived within a few miles of the Lincoln cabin when Abraham was born and Mrs. Dearing recalled carrying a dish of chicken broth to Nancy Hanks Lincoln a few days after she had brought her son into the world. A great-granddaughter of Mrs. Dearing is Mrs. Forrest Daniell, 3610 Ector street.

A daughter of Mrs. Dearing, Mrs. Rachford of Port Neches, is living in Port Neches.

MANY CABINS IN MEMORY OF ABRAHAM LINCOLN

A house built with sixty-one logs has become the best known home in all the universe. Within this log cabin, Abraham Lincoln was born on February 12, 1809. Three presidents of the United States during their respective administrations assisted in programs that looked forward to the permanent preservation of this cabin. President Theodore Roosevelt laid the cornerstone of the building which was to enclose it; President William Howard Taft was the principal speaker at the time the cabin was enshrined within the building; and President Woodrow Wilson accepted the shrine on behalf of the Nation.

Many replicas of the cabin have been built. In Denmark, one of these replicas stands in a city park to allow the youth of the city to visualize how the most humble may succeed. One of the most interesting replicas of the cabin stands in Milton, Massachusetts, on the estate of Miss Mary Bowditch Forbes. The first replica, however, was built in Foster Park, Fort Wayne, Indiana, by the Lincoln National Life Insurance Company. It is furnished in a primitive style, with corner cupboards, plain poster bed, drop-leaf table, fireplace, utensils and other pioneer furnishings.

The original cabin, now reconstructed in the Memorial Building at Hodgenville, is seventeen feet by thirteen feet, and eleven logs high to the eaves, thirteen logs to the ridgepole. It has one window and one door, both cut from the same side of the cabin. A stick chimney is built outside of the cabin wall at one end. There is no floor in the cabin, and the roof is made of long singles held in place by wooden pegs and weighted down by long poles.

Lincoln Memorial Cabin
Dedicated In Northwest

WENATCHEE, Wash.—(U.P.) — A cabin built as a memorial to Abraham Lincoln on a plain near here below a great stone face resembling that of the Civil War President has been dedicated.

The cabin, erected by the Washington unit of the Sons of Union Veterans, was built to the exact specifications as the one in which Lincoln was born at Hodgenville, Ky. Decades ago the site was the camping ground for an Indian pacifist leader, Chief Moses.

The stone face which overhangs the cabin is called Lincoln Rock because it bears such a likeness to the President. Sentinel Dec 8 1939

667 Fairfield Ave.
Bridgeport Conn.
May 27, 1938

Mr. Louis A. Warren
Care Lincoln National Life Insurance Co.
Fort Wayne, Indiana

My dear Mr. Warren: —

Bridgeport has several very
attractive parks, one bordering
on Long Island Sound, one through
which the Pequonnock river
flows, a new development called
"90 acres" which is entirely in-
land, and several smaller open
spaces.

It has been proposed that we
place a model of Abraham Lincoln's birthplace in one of these
parks.

I have visited our public library and read circular No. 349

describing the cabin and am
very anxious to obtain a copy.
Is it for sale?

Are there any legal restrictions
against our carrying out this
plan? If not is there a
pamphlet giving definite
information which would
assist us in carrying out
our plan? If so where can
it be obtained and what is
the cost?

Any suggestions you could
make will be appreciated.
We are anxious to start as
soon as possible so would
be glad to receive an early
reply.

Is the Lincoln Lore fur-
nished to libraries only or

are copies sent to public high schools? At what expense?

Awaiting your reply I am

Very truly yours

(Miss) Sara E. Goudren

Past Pres. Elias Howe Jr. M.R.C.

No. 53

May 31, 1938

Miss Sara E. Boudren
Past President Elias Howe, Jr.,W.R.C. #53
667 Fairfield Avenue
Bridgeport, Connecticut

My dear Madam:

        We are very glad to comply with your request for
a copy of Lincoln Lore No. 349 and we are also enclosing
copy of Lincoln Lore No. 381, which gives specific details
with reference to the building of the log cabin.

        You will also please find enclosed a photograph
of the log cabin, which also may be helpful in its
construction.

        We would be very glad indeed to place your name
on our mailing list for Lincoln Lore if you would be glad
to have it, and there would be no expense incurred by it.

                        Very truly yours,

LAW:EB   Director
Encs.(3)

667 Fairfield Ave.
Bridgeport, Conn
June 4th 193

Dr. Louis A. Warren
Fort Wayne, Indiana:

My dear Dr. Warren: -
Please accept my thanks for
the information you sent me
relative to the "Lincoln Log Cabin".
We are not yet sure that
the plan can be carried out
but feel greatly encouraged
by the attitude of our splendid
mayor Jasper McLevy.
We must now await the
action of the Board of Park
Commissioners which holds
a business meeting next
Tuesday, the president of

this board being Mr. Hilton
Barnum Seley, a grandson
of the one and only P.T. Barnum.
Mr. Seley has visited the Log
Cabin so can help us in many
ways.

I shall be very glad to have
my name on the mailing
list for "Lincoln Lore" and
would especially like to receive additional copies of Nos 349
and 381

Thanking you again for
your courtesy I am

Very truly yours
Sara E. Bowdren

June 9, 1938

Sara N. Boudren
667 Fairfield Avenue
Bridgeport, Connecticut

Dear Madam:

     We will be pleased indeed to place your name on
our mailing list to receive Lincoln Lore, and enclosed you
will please find extra copies of the bulletin which you
desire.

            Very truly yours,

                 Director

LAW:EB
Enc.(3)

Nichols and Nichols

Edmund Nichols
Edmund Nichols, Jr.

Law Offices
A.G. Bartlett Buil
215 West Seventh S
Los Angeles, Califo

June 10,1938

Lincoln National Life Foundation
Fort Wayne, Indiana

Gentlemen:

      The writer is a member of the Lincoln Fellowship of Southern California, and has been receiving the " Lincoln Lore " for the past two years or more. On July 27,1936,.there was sent out as No.381, a description with details of the Lincoln cabin. The last paragraph upon the page contained the following:-

      " The Lincoln National Life Foundation would be pleased to furnish a picture of the cabin to any group who anticipates building a replica."

      The Lincoln Fellowship, which had the pleasure of entertaining Dr. Warren while he was here last summer, has s ponsored a movement to have a replica of the Lincoln cabin erected at the entrance of the Lincoln Park in Los Angeles. This park already has a statue of Lincoln and we desire to have the two placed in a suitable location.

      The organization has taken the matter up with the Park Board and it is receiving favorable consideration . In a recent letter, the board requested a picture of the cabin together with the size, etc. In order that this may be supplied to the Board, will you be kind enough to send me a picture of the Lincoln cabin together with a copy of the issue of the Lincoln Lore under date of July 27,1936? This carries No. 381 and will be of material assistance to us in our work of presenting the matter to the Board, and will be greatly appreciated by our organization.

      Very sincerely yours ,

EN:am

June 16, 1938

Mr. Edmund Nichols
A. G. Bartlett Building
215 West Seventh Street
Los Angeles, California

My dear Mr. Nichols:

We are very glad indeed to comply with your
request for extra copies of Lincoln Lore No. 381 and
also a picture of the Lincoln cabin. We trust this
may be of help to you in the project you have in mind.

Very truly yours,

LAW:EB   Director

Cabin, Stone /1-2?-3?
Honor Lincoln

WENATCHEE, Wash. — (U.P.) — A cabin built as a memorial to Abraham Lincoln on a plain near here below a great stone face resembling that of the Civil war president has been dedicated.

The cabin, erected by the Washington unit of the Sons of Union Veterans, was built to the exact specifications as the one in which Lincoln was born at Hodgenville, Ky. Decades ago the site was the camping ground for an Indian pacifist leader, Chief Moses.

The stone face which overhangs the cabin is called Lincoln Rock because it bears such a likeness to the President.

LINCOLN
GOVERNMENT
LEAGUE
2408 MEDFORD ST.
LOS ANGELES, CAL.
"All Nations
Under one Flag"
— Lincoln

Los Angeles, California
December 12, 1939

Mr. Louis A. Warren
Editor, "Lincoln Lore"
Fort Wayne, Indiana

Dear Dr. Warren:

In Lincoln Park, Los Angeles, is an undeveloped hill which
would be an ideal location for a Lincoln shrine in the form of a
replica of Lincoln's birthplace, in which could be housed photo-
graphs, etc., of outstanding Lincoln landmarks, etc.

As President of the Lincoln Government League (founded
1927) I wrote to the Los Angeles Department of Parks and on
December 8, received the following:

"Dear Sir:
This will acknowledge your letter of November 6,
suggesting that a Lincoln Shrine in the form of a replica of
the Lincoln Log Cabin Birthplace be installed in Lincoln
Park.

Your letter was considered by the Board of Park Commissioners on December 7 and referred to the Superintendent
for investigation and report. Upon receipt of the report
and action thereon by the Board we will again communicate
with you.
Signed,
J.J. Hassett, secretary ."

I think it would be ideal to have the cabin constructed
out of our own redwood. I took the matter up with a large
West Coast lumber company relative to furnishing the material,
providing we can get the logs in the Lincoln Cabin measured and
numbered to aid in the construction. As that cabin has been
knocked down and errected time and again, no doubt they have
those specifications on hand. Could you give us some help along
this line?

Yours truly,
E.F. Rudeen
President, Lincoln Government
League
2408 Medford Street
Los Angeles, California

P.S. You might forward this letter to the Society in
charge of the Lincoln Log Cabin Shrine in Kentucky.

December 19, 1939

Mr. E. F. Rudeen
2408 Medford St.
Los Angeles, Calif.

My dear Mr. Rudeen:

You will please find enclosed a copy of Lincoln Lore No. 381 which gives you the exact dimensions of the cabin now enshrined in the Lincoln Memorial at Hodgenville, Kentucky.

We happen to have here in a park in Fort Wayne one of these replicas which our company constructed many years ago.

Very truly yours,

LAW:PW   Director
L.A.Warren

August 23, 1940

Mr. Erskine Kerr
1227 Boulevard
Lake Charles, La.

My dear Mr. Kerr:

With respect to the cabin shrine at Memorial Building in Hodgenville I think there has always been some doubt as to its genuineness although most of us have believed that it did contain a few of the old logs from the original cabin.

The Government is about to put out a publication which I think will be very frank in discussing just what is known about the old cabin. Personally I am of the opinion that although it has been greatly changed, the size is much smaller than the original, there are some of the old logs of the original birthplace cabin.

I had known of Mr. Robert Lincoln's reaction toward the cabin for many years and I think I know the source of this information, but I am not sure that this source of information is correct but I am very sure it was not his father who told him about the construction of the cabin.

It is quite true we have too many coats for Abraham Lincoln and all of them seem to be well documented. Just the other day I had a letter from a good woman who wanted to sell me the shawl that Lincoln wore that night. You might be interested in this bulletin which I enclose which was written some eight years ago and I expect the number of items could now be doubled from the information we have in our file.

I think most of the efforts which are made to claim genuineness are sincere in their purposes, most of the people relying on reminiscences rather than historical affirmations as sources for their stories. One by one, however, these various memorials are given historical background.

Thank you, indeed, for your information.

Very truly yours,

LAW:EB   Director
Encls.

Dear Sirs:

I understand you have material on Lincoln which you make available to the public — Do you have anything on the log cabins in which he lived — as my husband & I are trying to build a REAL "pioneer" (atmosphere) cabin. Information on interiors & exteriors are both welcome.

Sincerely

mrs. C. S. Hollingsworth
g. Postmaster
College, Alaska

14

POST CARD

Lincoln National Life

Fort Wayne

Indiana

Replica Cabin

March 17, 1950

Mrs. C.S. Hollingsworth
c/o Postmaster
College, Alaska

My dear Madam:

        You will please find attached a description
of the Lincoln cabin which now   the memorial at
Hodgenville, giving its exact dimensions. I think it
is about what you have reference to in your postcard
of February 7.

        My reply has been delayed by my absence from
the office on a long speaking itinerary.

                            Very truly yours,

LAW:EB   Director
Enc.

CHICAGO DAILY NEWS
Chicago, Ill.
Sept. 22, 1972

Abe cabin replica offers lessons

By Rob Warden

Chicago is getting a replica of the Abe Lincoln "birthplace" log cabin in Kentucky.

It will offer schoolchildren a lesson in both history and inflation.

The cost is about $17,200. That includes $4,200 for oak timbers and other materials. The labor is $13,000.

PEPPER Construction Co. is building the replica in a new wing of the Chicago Historical Society Museum, at the edge of Lincoln Park on the northeast corner of North Av. and Clark St.

The "original" cabin stands near Hodgenville, Ky., at the Lincoln Birthplace National Historic Site.

No one knows for sure what the original cost.

One thing more certain about the Hodgenville cabin is that it's most surely a fake.

"It was pawned off on the people who put it there," said Paul Angle, a Lincoln Historian and Historical Society consultant. The cabin was put there in 1909, on the 100th anniversary of Lincoln's birth.

CHICAGO'S replica will be a feature display in a new Lincoln gallery at the museum. The gallery also will feature dioramas of episodes in Lincoln's life, including the Stephen A. Douglas debates and signing of the Emancipation Proclamation.

The gallery, costing a total of $70,000, is expected to open Nov. 1.

EVEN the fireplace was constructed of logs and an open
fire would have burnt the building to the ground.

REPLICA of Lincoln's cabin was constructed with square logs, just as the original
was. Kids said round logs are a 20th century innovation.

Kids Build Copy Of Lincoln's Home — Can't Figure How He Studied At Night

It's nice to think about Abraham Lincoln as a youngster struggling each night to study his lessons by the light of a fire in his log cabin.

But it took a group of high school kids from San Marino, Calif., to discover this probably isn't true.

The students from Southwestern Academy recently completed a replica of the log cabin Lincoln was born and raised in.

During the process of researching and building the cabin, they discovered a lot of misconceptions about Lincoln.

"He couldn't have studied by firelight because the pioneers never had an open fire in the fireplace of their cabins," said Kenneth Veronda, the school's director.

The students discovered that the fireplaces of cabins like Lincoln's were made of logs, too, and they would have burned if an open flame had been used.

"Instead, pioneers kept hot coals in the fireplace all the time to provide heat for cooking and to warm the cabin," he explained.

Instead, the students concluded Lincoln probably read in the early evening outside, especially in the spring and summer months when the sun sets later.

"The students spent hundreds of hours reading books and writings from the time of Lincoln to discover how the pioneers lived," Veronda explained.

Two students spent a week at the Lincoln Memorial in Kentucky where the actual cabin believed to be Lincoln's childhood home is preserved.

"They took measurements, notes on construction techniques, and studied documents. With all of this information they figured they could build a cabin like Lincoln's," he said.

Originally the purpose in building the cabin was for the students to gain some insight into how hard the settler's life really was and not to destroy any of the folklore surrounding Lincoln. But finding the errors they did prompted the students to look even deeper.

"They found the early settlers didn't use round logs to build their cabins," Veronda said. "They squared the logs off because you can't stack them very well even when they're notched. The idea of building a cabin with round logs is a 20th century concept."

They also discovered that even large pioneering families built small cabins. The Lincoln cabin for instance is barely 12' x 16' and was just one big room. But even that took pioneers about six weeks to build.

"There's a story about Lincoln having read a book one night and when finished he supposedly stuck it in a space between the log of the wall. It rained that night and the book was ruined by the water," he said.

"It's doubtful such a thing could have happened. It's very unlikely there was a break between the logs large enough to slip a book into. The logs were square not round and very tight fitting."

However the notion that Lincoln was self-educated is very likely true.

"He apparently had only 1 1/2 years of formal schooling from about the second to about half of the third grade. The rest he managed to get on his own," Veronda sa.d.

How were these high school students able to find such glaring errors when the experts who write textbooks and encyclopedias have not?

"For one thing they ignored most of the material written in this century about Lincoln and instead went back into the 19th century material," Veronda said of his students.

"They also researched writings from around the time of Lincoln but not necessarily about Lincoln to get information."

Veronda and the students at the school hope that by building the cabin which duplicates Lincoln's, and by conducting the minute research they did, he still stands as an extraordinary president without having gone to extraordinary means as a youngster.